Oceans and Seas

Indian Ocean

John F. Prevost

ABDO Publishing Company

visit us at
www.abdopub.com

Published by ABDO Publishing Company, 4940 Viking Drive, Edina, Minnesota 55435.
Copyright © 2003 by Abdo Consulting Group, Inc. International copyrights reserved in
all countries. No part of this book may be reproduced in any form without written
permission from the publisher.

Printed in the United States.

Photo Credits: Corbis

Contributing Editors: Kate A. Conley, Kristin Van Cleaf, Kristianne E. Vieregger
Art Direction & Maps: Neil Klinepier

Library of Congress Cataloging-in-Publication Data

Prevost, John F.
    Indian Ocean / John F. Prevost.
        p. cm. -- (Oceans and seas)
    Includes index.
    Summary: Surveys the origin, geological borders, climate, water, plant and animal
life, and economic and ecological aspects of the Indian Ocean.
    ISBN 1-57765-094-8
    1. Indian Ocean--Juvenile literature. [1. Indian Ocean.] I. Title. II. Series: Prevost,
    John F. Oceans and seas.
GC721.P74 1998
551.46'7--dc21   98-12653
                                                          CIP
                                                           AC

Contents

The Indian Ocean

The Indian Ocean is the world's third-largest ocean. Its waters cover about 26 million square miles (67 million sq km). It lies between Africa, Asia, Australia, and the Southern Ocean.

Unlike the Atlantic and Pacific Oceans, the Indian Ocean is mostly south of the **equator**. On the north, it is enclosed by India and Asia. This creates a distinctive climate in this region.

The Indian Ocean contains **seas**, bays, and gulfs. Some main seas are the Red Sea and the Arabian Sea. The Persian Gulf, the Gulf of Aden, and the Bay of Bengal are also parts of this ocean.

The Indian Ocean has not always looked as it does today. Millions of years ago, there was only one ocean, Panthalassa. It surrounded the only continent, Pangaea. About 200 million years ago, Pangaea began breaking apart. Today's continents formed from the pieces. The new continents split Panthalassa into today's oceans.

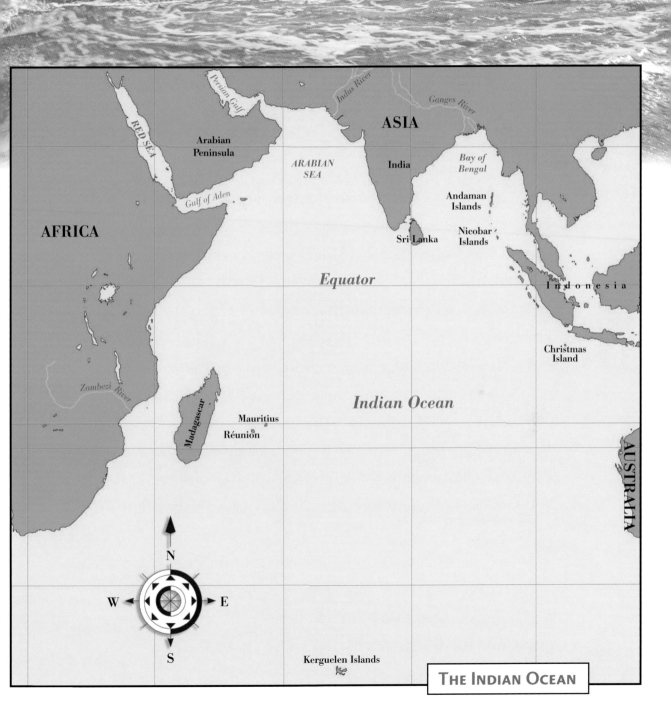

THE INDIAN OCEAN

Beneath the Waves

The Indian Ocean's floor has a narrow **continental shelf**. Beyond the shelf lie ridges, hills, **plateaus**, and basins. The deepest point is Sunda Deep, in the Java Trench. It lies 24,452 feet (7,453 m) below **sea level**.

An underwater mountain range runs through the center of the Indian Ocean. It forms an upside-down Y shape. It begins as the Mid-Indian Ridge in the north. Farther south, it splits into the Southeast and Southwest Indian Ridges. **Seafloor spreading** occurs along these ridges.

Ninety East Ridge is one of the ocean's most distinctive features. It runs north and south near the Bay of Bengal. At 2,800 miles (4,506 km) long, it is the longest straight ridge on Earth.

Islands in the Indian Ocean are either tops of volcanoes or pieces of the continents. Madagascar is the world's fourth-largest island. Other islands include Sri Lanka, Christmas Island, and the Kerguelen Islands.

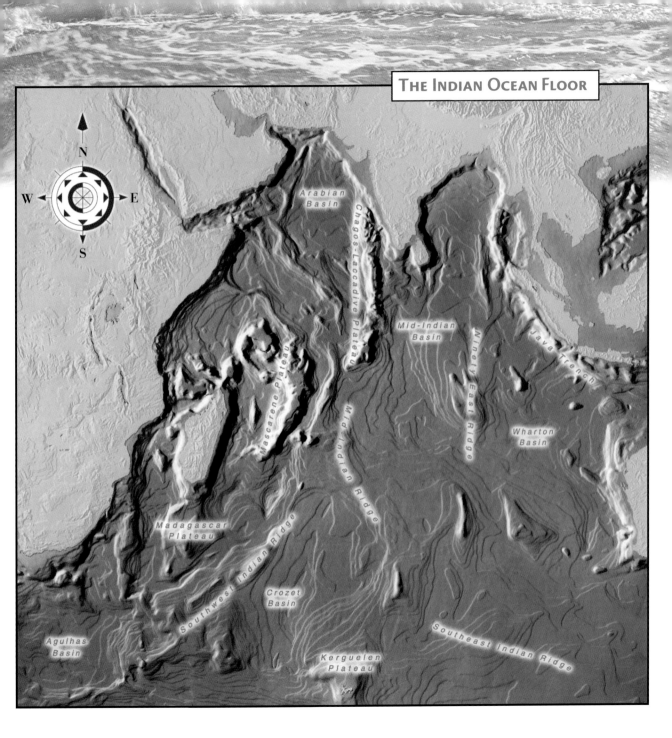

Climate

The Indian Ocean has a distinctive climate. Seasonal winds called monsoons strongly affect the weather. They are caused by differences between land and ocean temperatures. The strongest monsoons occur in India and southern Asia.

During the northeast monsoon, the land is cooler than the ocean. This causes the wind to blow from the land to the ocean. It occurs between November and April and brings dry weather.

The southwest monsoon is between May and October. During this time, the ocean is cooler than the land. This causes the wind to blow wet air from the ocean to the land. It brings large amounts of rain to India and southern Asia.

The Indian Ocean also has other types of wind. The trade winds blow near the **equator**. They blow steadily southwestward and are strongest between June and September.

Tropical cyclones also form over the Indian Ocean. They form over warm water and generally move westward. These storms have strong, rotating winds moving at least 74 miles per hour (119 km/h). They are most common just before and after the southwest monsoon.

Tropical cyclones can cause huge, damaging waves.

Water

The Indian Ocean's water arrives through rain, and rivers such as the Zambezi, Ganges, and Indus. The hydrologic cycle moves this water back and forth between the land and the ocean.

Salt and other **dissolved** minerals are a part of the Indian Ocean's water. They enter the ocean through rivers and deep **rifts** in the ocean floor. Gases, such as oxygen and nitrogen, are also dissolved in ocean water.

Streams called currents flow through the Indian Ocean's water. South of the **equator**, currents flow counterclockwise. North of the equator, currents flow clockwise. But during the monsoon seasons, the currents north of the equator reverse direction.

The Indian Ocean also has upwelling, which is also caused by monsoons. Upwelling occurs when ocean water travels up from the ocean bottom. This water is colder than the surface water, and full of ocean-floor **nutrients**.

Tides are the rise and fall of the oceans. Gravity pulls ocean water toward the moon. The area facing the moon, and the area facing directly away, have high tide. Low tide occurs in the areas in between. Most tides in the Indian Ocean occur twice a day as Earth rotates.

THE HYDROLOGIC CYCLE

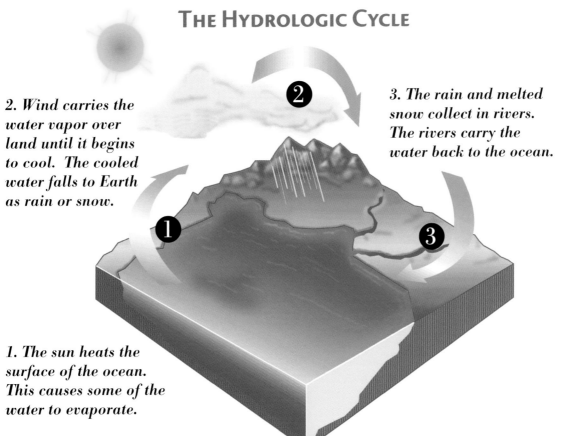

2. Wind carries the water vapor over land until it begins to cool. The cooled water falls to Earth as rain or snow.

3. The rain and melted snow collect in rivers. The rivers carry the water back to the ocean.

1. The sun heats the surface of the ocean. This causes some of the water to evaporate.

Plants

Plants in the Indian Ocean need sunlight for **photosynthesis**. So most plants live either in the surface waters or in the shallow waters near shore. There, the sunlight can still reach them. Ocean plants either float or are attached to the ocean floor.

Sea horses wrap their tails around algae growing on the ocean floor.

Phytoplankton make up the majority of the ocean's plants. These tiny, free-floating plants drift in the currents. They are the base of the ocean's **food chain**. In the Indian Ocean, phytoplankton are abundant due to upwelling. The **nutrients** brought to the surface are a source of food.

Large algae, also called seaweeds, grow in the oceans. They usually grow on the ocean bottom, within 330 feet (101 m) of the surface. Due to the Indian Ocean's warm water, lots of red algae grow there. Coralline red algae are a part of many coral **reefs** in the ocean's warmer areas.

Mangroves grow along the shore. Mangrove trees have pale yellow flowers and grow to be about 30 feet (9 m) tall. They have long, exposed roots that reach out into the water. These roots support the soil in coastal areas.

A mangrove tree's roots stick out above the water in order to get air.

Animals

Hundreds of animal species live in or around the Indian Ocean. Ocean animals either float in the currents or swim. Some also live on the ocean floor.

Zooplankton are animals that float. Most types of zooplankton are too small to see. They eat phytoplankton. Copepods are common forms of Indian Ocean zooplankton. Often, larger ocean animals eat zooplankton.

Animals that swim are called nekton. They move freely through the water. Nekton include whales, squid, dolphins, dugongs, **sea** turtles, and fish. Coelacanths, fish once thought to be extinct, have only been found in the Indian Ocean.

Benthos are animals living on the ocean floor. They include small animals, called coral, that live in colonies. They live in shallow, warm water. Coral have hard skeletons, which build up to form **reefs**. The reefs are an **ecosystem** of animals and plants. Sponges, mollusks, sea urchins, and many brightly colored fish are just a few coral reef animals.

A school of fish swims near the Seychelles Islands.

Trade & Exploration

People have used the Indian Ocean for thousands of years. The ancient Egyptians sailed its waters as early as 2300 B.C. The Greek historian Herodotus mentions Indian Ocean explorations around 600 B.C.

Writings of Arab and Persian sailors in the A.D. 800s through the 1400s contain details on navigating the ocean. They tell how to use the winds and currents. They also describe islands and coasts. People used this information to aid trade between countries.

Portuguese sailor Vasco da Gama sailed around the tip of Africa in 1497. He was the first European to discover this route to the Indian Ocean. Dutch sailor Abel Tasman explored the Indian Ocean between 1642 and 1644. He was the first European to see Tasmania.

In the 1900s, scientists began exploring the Indian Ocean's water and floor. Ocean life also continues to be a topic of discovery. Today, there is still much opportunity for exploration.

For hundreds of years, traders have used small ships called dhows to travel between Asian and African ports.

Indian Ocean Today

Today, people continue to make use of the Indian Ocean's many resources. The fishing industry, however, is fairly small. The warm climate causes fish to spoil quickly. But people from many countries still catch shrimp, tuna, billfish, snappers, mackerel, and other fish.

Miners drill for minerals beneath the ocean floor. Tin, zircon, manganese, and natural gas are all valuable. However, many of these resources are difficult to reach. For this reason, they have not yet been heavily mined.

Large reserves of oil were discovered under the Persian Gulf's floor in the 1930s. Today, it is the world's largest oil-producing region. Almost 40 percent of the world's offshore **petroleum** comes from the Persian Gulf.

The Indian Ocean is also important to shipping traffic. The many countries surrounding the ocean trade iron, coal, rubber, tea, and other goods across the waters.

The Challis Venture *is an oil tanker attached to an oil well off the coast of Australia. The oil flows up through pipes and into the ship's bow. Other ships then collect the oil.*

Environment

People have used the Indian Ocean's resources for many years. But much of this activity has damaged its waters.

Mining for fertilizer on many islands has removed much of the plant life. Many native plant species were destroyed as a result. This has also hurt the animals that depend on these plants. The introduction of species not native to these environments has also upset the **ecosystem**.

Water pollution is a serious threat to the Indian Ocean. Cities and industries create waste, which pollutes river and ocean water. The contaminated water kills much of the phytoplankton and zooplankton. It also threatens many other plant and animal species, including coral **reef** communities.

Petroleum mining has also been a large contributor to this pollution. Accidental oil spills have harmed many plant and animal species. Then, in an act of war in 1991, Iraqi

Oil coated the coastline for miles after the oil spill in 1991.

soldiers purposely dumped more than 12 million barrels of oil into the Persian Gulf. The oil killed thousands of plants and animals. This is the worst oil spill in history.

Today, many agencies are working to protect the Indian Ocean. They are researching cleanup methods and other ways to protect this ocean for the future.

Glossary

continental shelf - the shallow area around each continent.

dissolve - to break down and spread evenly throughout a liquid.

ecosystem - a community of organisms and their environment functioning as one unit.

equator - an imaginary circle around the middle of Earth.

food chain - an arrangement of plants and animals in a community. Each plant or animal feeds on other plants or animals in a certain order. For example, phytoplankton are eaten by small fish, small fish are eaten by large fish, and large fish are eaten by humans.

nutrients - vitamins and minerals that all living things need to survive.

petroleum - a thick, yellowish-black oil. It is the source of gasoline.

photosynthesis - the process by which green plants use light energy, carbon dioxide, and water to make food and oxygen.

plateau - a raised area of flat land.

reef - a chain of rocks or coral, or a ridge of sand, near the water's surface.

rift - a long, deep, narrow crack.

sea - a body of water that is smaller than an ocean and is almost completely surrounded by land.

sea level - the average height of all the oceans. It is often used to measure height or depth, with sea level as zero feet.

seafloor spreading - a process that forms new seafloor.

How Do You Say That?

algae - AL-jee
coelacanth - SEE-luh-kanth
copepod - KOH-puh-pahd
cyclone - SI-klohne
Herodotus - hih-RAH-duh-tuhs
hydrologic - hi-druh-LAH-jihk

Pangaea - pan-JEE-uh
Panthalassa - pan-THA-luh-suh
phytoplankton - fi-toh-PLANGK-tuhn
Vasco da Gama - VAS-koh dah-GA-muh
zooplankton - zoh-uh-PLANGK-tuhn

Web Sites

Would you like to learn more about the Indian Ocean? Please visit
www.abdopub.com to find up-to-date Web site links about the
Indian Ocean and its animals. These links are routinely monitored
and updated to provide the most current information available.

Index